BOOKS BY MONA VAN DUYN

Near Changes

For Joann, with all good wishes,
Mona Van Duyn

NEAR CHANGES

POEMS

Mona Van Duyn

ALFRED A. KNOPF

New York

1992

THIS IS A BORZOI BOOK
PUBLISHED BY ALFRED A. KNOPF, INC.

POEMS IN THESE PAGES HAVE APPEARED IN

The Atlantic: "Late Loving."

Grand Street: "The Ferris Wheel," "Last Words of Pig No. 6707," "Headlines."

Memorial for David Kalstone: "For David Kalstone."

Missouri Women Writers: "The Insight Lady of St. Louis on Zoos."

The New Republic: "Misers," "Double Sonnet for Minimalists."

The New Yorker: "First Trip Through the Automatic Carwash," "Addendum for a Future Visit to the Hecht Study" (under the title "Gardens").

Ploughshares: "Mockingbird Month."

Poetry: "Views," "Near Changes," "A Bouquet of Zinnias," "To a Friend Who Threw Away Hair Dyes," "In Bed With a Book," "Falling in Love at Sixty-Five," "The Burning of Yellowstone," "Glad Heart at the Supermarket," "Sonnet for Minimalists."

The Poetry Bag: "Birthstones."

River City: "The Block."

River Styx: "At the New Orleans Zoo."

The St. Louis Post-Dispatch: "Cotton Wagons."

The Yale Review: "Journal Jottings," "Pigeon Eggs," "Memoir."

I wish to thank the N.E.A., under whose grant many of these poems were written.

Library of Congress Cataloging-in-Publication Data

Van Duyn, Mona.
  Near changes: poems/by Mona Van Duyn.—1st ed.
      p.   cm.
    ISBN 0–394–58444–9
    ISBN 0–679–72909–7 (pbk.)
    I. Title.
  PS3543.A563N4   1990
  811'.54–dc20

89–43358
CIP

Manufactured in the United States of America
Published February 26, 1992
Second Printing, July 1992

For JARVIS *and for* MY FRIENDS,
who fill to the brim a life empty of family

CONTENTS

I V

Near Changes

BIRTHSTONES

When I was young and we were poor
my mother showed me a ring some old love gave her,
and said, "I'll have your birthstone set in it."

And said, "Don't ever lose it. The jeweler
offered to sell me half-glass, half-emerald,
but I'm giving you the real jewel."

I wore it as if she had given me the world.
I had no notion what things cost.
I thought she'd love me if I could be good at last,

but I never was. When I thought I knew her face
I told her I realized that stone was glass.
She blushed, and said the jeweler must have lied.

I looked in books to find out how to feel.
Then, holding them cheap, I tried an exchange of rings.
My new one tested real.

And on I went, and learned to recognize
the faintest glimmer of pure green
in a hand's clasp, or a pair of eyes,

and out came carats of green from a guarded mine
in grateful exchange, and back came green in turn.
When I looked again I was grown,

and my fingers were decked with rings, and still more green
exchanges came, and we dropped them on the ground
as our hands filled and boxes filled,

and they roll and shine as far as I can see.
Dazzled I walk the world my mother gave me,
whose stony streets are paved with emerald.

[1966]

I

FALLING IN LOVE AT SIXTY-FIVE

It is like the first and last time I tried a Coleman
for reading in bed in Maine. Too early the camp
went dark for fossil habits, no longer could candleflame
convince my eyes, and I lit that scary lamp.
Instant outcry came from the savage white light
of the mantles, as if a star had been brought down
out of space and trapped by the unchinked logs of the bedroom,
roaring its threat to explode the walls and be gone,
or as if the lamp could tell time and knew that one tongue
was no longer enough to speak with, it must double its blare,
overwhelm two senses at once, that the jaded heart
might burst into ravished applause for its *son et lumière*.

Perched on a pile of books on the seat of a chair
drawn to the head of the bed, the lamp called out
the guilty years and shamed them for cracks and shrivels
that bent the patient, scabbed logs of the walls and ceiling.
Then I opened a book whose every radiant page
was illuminated in colors of lightning and thunder
by the quick-witted lamp in its artistry of rage.
The book and the lamp fused to one voice, whose sense
became mine, strokes of a slow, rhythmic broom
swept a dusty pith that seemed to lie still until
some other sense told me that there were wings in the room.

In one much earlier year I had fallen asleep
in the meadow, head near bright heights of fireweed, fireweed
strewn on my chest from a hand that let go its bouquet,
and had wakened at eyelash touches, the delicate need
of five blue butterflies that found me in bloom.
Now, striking my neck and cheeks, came the first
wave of this late invasion, three flying bugs
that hit me, lit, flew again, hit, an outburst
the lamp had called for through log-gaps and screenholes, then
more entered the air, winged in gray, brown, dun,
and more, as I tried to read on, in the muted shades
brushed on by sundown's dimming imagination.

7

Falling in Love at Sixty-five
Beetle-bodied or light as moths they came
and, big and small, bombed the lit skin of face,
arms, shoulders, rested, crawled, unfurled, and sent
the blind wanting that stuffed full each one's carapace
in a clicking crash at the lampglass, then crazily flew
back to me, the bared part of me becoming a plan
for plates of an insect book whose specimens
rearranged themselves fiercely over and over again.
For as long as the lantern lasted they would have kept coming,
as if the grave darkness had smiled at that tiny dawn
and had hurled them in fistfuls straight at the speaking light
in answer to what was being insisted upon.

LATE LOVING

"What Christ was saying, what he meant [in the story of Mary and Martha] was that the pleasures of that hair, that ointment, must be taken. Because the accidents of death would deprive us soon enough. We must not deprive ourselves, our loved ones, of the luxury of our extravagant affections. We must not try to second-guess death by refusing to love the ones we loved...." Mary Gordon, FINAL PAYMENTS

If in my mind I marry you every year
it is to calm an extravagance of love
with dousing custom, for it flames up fierce
and wild whenever I forget that we live
in double rooms whose temperature's controlled
by matrimony's turned-down thermostat.
I need the mnemonics, now that we are old,
of oath and law in re-memorizing that.
Our dogs are dead, our child never came true.
I might use up, in my weak-mindedness,
the whole human supply of warmth on you
before I could think of others and digress.
"Love" is finding the familiar dear.
"In love" is to be taken by surprise.
Over, in the shifty face you wear,
and over, in the assessments of your eyes,
you change, and with new sweet or barbed word
find out new entrances to my inmost nerve.
When you stand at the stove it's I who am most stirred.
When you finish work I rest without reserve.
Daytimes, sometimes, our three-legged race seems slow.
Squabbling onward, we chafe from being so near.
But all night long we lie like crescents of Velcro,
turning together till we re-adhere.
Since you, with longer stride and better vision,
more clearly see the finish line, I stoke
my hurrying self, to keep it in condition,
with light and life-renouncing meals of smoke.

Late Loving

> As when a collector scoops two Monarchs in
> at once, whose fresh flights to and from each other
> are netted down, so in vows I re-imagine
> I re-invoke what keeps us stale together.
> What you try to give is more than I want to receive,
> yet each month when you pick up scissors for our appointment
> and my cut hair falls and covers your feet I believe
> that the house is filled again with the odor of ointment.

FIRST TRIP THROUGH THE AUTOMATIC CARWASH

Clamped to another will, the self in its glass
begins a slow, tugged slide, toward what clarifying?
First the world had rolled in clinging crystal, then a deface
of gripping gray was spread by others, drying
to smear and mottle that threatened her own movement.
This strange detour is a clear necessity.
Drenching and blindness signal the first improvement.
This much is familiar, natural as rain would be
after the lights blow out, filling any pane
or cornea with hopelessness that will go away
after its little havoc, disclosing sunshine,
and how long it will last no one is expected to say.
But now this snail-spin, in neutral, sends her in a fierce
forest whose long dark leaves wrap her in a wild
and waving threat, a typhoon that is all hers,
swabbing to get in, as the storms of a child
threaten the very skin of the child, its frail
shell of self-regard. In mercy, this ends.
And now begins a scouring away at the braille
of outward features, a terrible wish that contends
with the speaking shapes of what she is and has been,
a spinning scrub that seems to aim for bare bone.
To destroy the customary in order to let in
something unwitnessed yet, and be wholly alone
for its witnessing, seems to be the aim of this stage.
What is whirling away? The long wedlock,
its bolt ground loose? Or the whole safe cage
of sane connections? Or, from beneath, a bedrock
trust in words, their grounding for her very name?
Whatever is left is suddenly released, a few
deep breaths can be taken before she's jerked to the same
dark jungle of thrashing fronds as before, but with new
insistence. Something refuses to be withstood.
Its untamed, zigzag, dark rubbing will break through.

First Trip Through the Automatic Carwash
    You *will* change, it squeaks, I replace old selfhood.
    As the newly beloved asks of the lover, Who?,
    as nouns rinsed of meaning ask What?, as in panic and daze
    the patient asks Where?, she strains for a shape to define.
    Whatever it is will enter everywhere, rephrase
    everything. At the last moment it lifts toward design.
    The heart makes its presence known, disheveled but whole,
    by jogging in place, lithely, at light's surprise.
    A hoot from behind makes her shift to self-control,
    and the muddle of everywhere falls on her clearing eyes.

VIEWS

I fly all the time, and still I'm afraid to fly.
I need to keep both feet on the ground, the earth
within reach of my eyes. In airports I comfort myself
by assessing others—look at that handsome necktie,
the weave of that suit, the portfolio, (people of worth
are going to be on this plane) the pearls on that shelf
of expensive bosom, the hairdresser's art! All this
tells my shuddering spirit that God wouldn't tip
my seatmates, all these important people, from sight.
Once the stewardess passed the word that Liz
would be joined in Rome by Richard Burton, who was up
in First Class. I have never felt so safe on a flight.

SECOND POET:

I too fly all the time, and still I tremble.
I arrive too early and sit there sweating and cold.
I read at a book but can't make out what it means.
I look around at the others as they assemble
and make a collection of the dowdy old,
backpacking young, slouched in their dusty jeans,
men who have business suits of the wrong size on,
Frizzled Hair, Greasy Hair and Drooping Hem.
Humbly they live and humbly they will die—
this scroungiest bunch of people I've ever laid eyes on.
Surely God has no special fate in mind for *them*,
I tell myself, like a plane falling out of the sky.

AT THE NEW ORLEANS ZOO

for Viktor

A four-legged bouquet of black peonies on tan hide
in configuration never to be repeated in the world
rising to a peak, a periscope of bloom, that holds a little tufted head
six feet high, he stands perfectly still and stares,
"charming, curious and unafraid," at the small two-legged crowd
staring back on the other side of his fenced zoo field,
perfectly modelled miniature of the huge other, who, some distance
    away,
"tallest animal in the world," bends down from sixteen to twenty feet
to browse on bushes and heaped up fodder.
"He is two days old," the people around us tell one another
and, pointing their own ice-cream-licking young at him,
they cry out over and over, "Look at the baby giraffe!"

Does he remember how precipitously he came to his ground?
How all through his birth his mother stood, and his head and neck
entered the strange air; how the contractions grew stronger,
shoved out his shoulders, then, more quickly, the rest of his body,
and he fell headfirst to the earth from five and a half feet
from the warm, cushiony waters, breaking the umbilical cord,
landing "with a thud"? He looks at us only, it seems, in wonder.

Fifteen minutes after his fall he got to his feet
and the lofty neck lifted the eyes toward that high view
which, with a fast gallop, is his sole safeguard
in the carnivorous world. His most dangerous predator is man.
For a month he will run and scamper, "kicking up his legs,"
then his playing will stop and he'll take on for life
his adult air "of quiet self-possession," meanwhile, to reach manhood,
having to grow, shoot up, sometimes nine inches in a single week.
Sleeping in his nature is no command to kill, only the giraffe bull's
"main goal in life—to pass on his genetic material,"
for in a herd he would try for dominance nonviolently
with a necking match, twining and untwining his neck
with that of another bull, in a sexual fight he would swing his head

"like a sledgehammer," ducking the headblows of the other bull,
until one of them fell, or was knocked unconscious or ran away,
the winner gaining the right to the estrous female.

Now something stirs in the mother and she leaves her grazing,
crosses the field to the infant, who has not moved,
who, as she nears, becomes smaller and smaller, a Noah's Ark toy,
and leans down and licks him. Instantly he turns his head from us
and moves up against her, nuzzling her side.
Bonding is taking place. He is not alone. They belong to each other.

Camelopard, the Greeks called him, taking him to be
a cross between creatures, the Bushmen painted him on rocks,
the ancient Egyptians drew him on tomb walls.
His existence could not be believed by Europeans
until two hundred years ago when he came as a gift to kings,
the gift of his graces, a "token of goodwill and peace."
An early explorer to Africa wrote that his strongest reaction
was "a feeling of pity for such beautiful
and utterly helpless creatures . . . who are perfectly defenceless."

The human children are restless, reluctantly we all move on,
saying at our best to the baby, "Welcome! When the cord broke
your 'dignity, aloofness, overwhelming gentleness'
fell into our bumbling hands.
May we learn to be, before it's too late for us both.
what your mild genes, at the top of the flowery neck, told you you
    saw."

PIGEON EGGS

for Peggy

"Some days, these days, the world's too hot to handle,
or cold, I guess I mean, too cold to kindle.

The next-door neighbor called: 'Peggy, your cats
your three damned cats have killed a rabbit!' That's

in the morning, it was lying in her back yard.
I got the spade—when it's dead it isn't hard—

but it moved, it was still alive! I took it home
on the spade, and waited with it till Howard came,

because Jeremy's had our Merc since he totalled his.
The rabbit was squeaking but Howard couldn't face

it either, so I borrowed the neighbor's Corvette
and drove the rabbit on the spade to the vet

for a shot. Coming home, at the busiest time of day,
a poodleish dog was running every-which-way

in the traffic, so I pulled to the side and got out
and dodged the cars and chased it down all right

and carried it into the car. Thank God for a tag!
I found the place, nobody home, closed the dog

in the back fenced yard and went home to have a drink.
Howard was playing Bach. Surely, you'd think,

my day was over, but you're wrong. My Bert,
my big yellow cat, had something that was hurt

outside the kitchen window. I chased him away
and it was a pigeon. You know what they always say,

things come in threes. I keep a box for birds
in the basement. I tell you I simply don't have words

for what happened next. I looked in the evening and there
was the pigeon, still alive, and I washed my hair

and did the dishes and straightened and went to bed,
and in the morning there was the pigeon, dead,

but before she died she had laid an egg. And it
was there in the box, stone cold. I thought, *Bullshit*!

How could I help but think of another time?
It was the same, but it was not the same.

We live, but our lives go on beyond our hands.
We tell, but we tell to no one who understands.

In our youth I put a pigeon in the box.
The world was hot, with the charming heat of sex,

and before the pigeon died she laid an egg.
The egg was warm when I found it. Mona, I beg

to defend that windowed world. I put it between
my breasts—the warm pigeon egg—all I had seen

and felt led me to believe in the coming birth.
I believed—and believe—I tell you for what it's worth.

I hardly knew the world and its funny ways.
Then Howie came home and hugged me! Those were the days!"

IN BED WITH A BOOK

In police procedurals they are dying all over town,
the life ripped out of them, by gun, bumper, knife,
hammer, dope, etcetera, and no clues at all.
All through the book the calls come in: body found
in bed, car, street, lake, park, garage, library,
and someone goes out to look and write it down.
Death begins life's whole routine to-do
in these stories of our fellow citizens.

Nobody saw it happen, or everyone saw,
but can't remember the car. What difference does it make
when the child will never fall in love, the girl will never
have a child, the man will never see a grandchild, the old maid
will never have another cup of hot cocoa at bedtime?
Like life, the dead are dead, their consciousness,
as dear to them as mine to me, snuffed out.
What has mind to do with this, when the earth is bereaved?

I lie, with my dear ones, holding a fictive umbrella,
while around us falls the real and acid rain.
The handle grows heavier and heavier in my hand.
Unlike life, tomorrow night under the bedlamp
by a quick link of thought someone will find out why,
and the policemen and their wives and I will feel better.
But all that's toward the end of the book. Meantime, tonight,
without a clue I enter sleep's little rehearsal.

II

NEAR CHANGES

from "The Year's Top Trivia,"
SANFORD TELLER *Information Please Almanac*, 1979

"Bob Holt, a 20-year-old Seattle man,
was quietly walking on a downtown street,
disguised as a mallard duck,
when he was—for no apparent reason—
attacked by a husky, 6-foot-tall
bearded stranger.
The perpetrator spun him around by one wing,
tore off his duck bill,
hit him over the head with it,
and ran away.
Holt, who was dressed as a duck
to promote a local radio station,
had no explanation for the incident.
He told police,
'I didn't speak to him.
I didn't flap my wings
or do anything like that.' "

Is this trivia, after all,
or a profound story?
The gods used to do it,
to themselves and to mortals,
sometimes in mercy,
sometimes out of blind and merciless power,
but the rest of us only yearn in odd moments
of our fixed lives for the sense of it,
of how it would feel to be bull or swan
or obsessively weaving spider or even
the plucked and plundered
tree of bay,
for "Emerging from one's own self . . . ," says Llosa,
"is a way . . . of experiencing
the risks of freedom."
With the help of paper feathers

supplied by a local radio station,
settling into his new shape,
having become green-headed, rufous-breasted,
with bold white neckring and yellow bill,
walking quietly along,
a Seattle man began to turn avian
on a downtown street,
though the metamorphosis was only half completed
since he could not quite say later,
"I didn't quack at him,"
but could say to fact-finders, "I didn't flap my wings
or do anything like that."

And the bearded stranger?
Prescient as Leda, he sensed the presence
which to others was not apparent,
and was only protecting his nest,
the brick and concrete of Sears and service stations
where the arm that ends in four fingers
and an opposable thumb
at one touch of a button
warms and cools the vulnerable flesh
and the brain in its dear, lip-voiding box of language
and lights the concealments of space
and brings forth the cadence of cars
and Beethoven to cover
the soundless spin of the globe
whose button is beyond its reach,
lest that nest return, at the wingéd touch
of the human imagination,
which transforms past belief,
sometimes in mercy,
sometimes in blind mercilessness,
to vast and silent waters
toward whose reedy edge
Bob Holt was coasting in for a landing,
without flapping his wings.

TO A FRIEND WHO THREW AWAY HAIR DYES

Surely history's seen a happy ruler!
Tell me the long wait that breaks the pride
and will, yet may end in mastery, is not vain,
that Time may love and take for royal bride
his humblest servant, and in exchange I'll tell you
that the heart's multitudes lower their eyes and bow down
at their first sight on the balcony of a beautiful,
brilliant head wearing its first cold crown.

ON A MAJOLICA SUNFLOWER PLATE
AMERICAN, EARLY 1880's

for J. and P.

Near to the sun, the sunflower faces him,
held high on stem-stilts that outgrew all shade,
her face the food of song, death's antonym.

Even in Kansas, where no clouds can dim
the fire of his sky-long raging, unafraid,
though near to the sun, the sunflower faces him,

for in that Heartland, counting Time's hot, grim
steps that blister the green to black has made
her face the food of song, death's antonym.

Thinking his rage mere passion's pseudonym
destroyed each fragile Icarus who strayed
near to the sun. Yet the sunflower faces him,

a lifted plate filled to its golden rim,
seeding the sky with notes the earth mislaid,
her face the food of song. When death's antonym

goes winging south to the Golden Clime, each hymn
to the god from Heartland's cooling sky will fade
till, near to the sun, a new sunflower faces him,
her face the food of song, death's antonym.

THE BALLOON GLOBE

Knowing its nature, its soap-bubble fragility
that any Great Dictator of Metaphor
could toss about with a fingertip in a Chaplin ballet,
one knows at the same time how weighty a symbol
has entered the house and drifted onto a massive table
already bearing, shelved underneath, its rows of reading,
unabridged language, albums of past journeys and photoed friendships,
on its top a stack of the quarterly topical and a tropical palm
towering over some modest little pots of bloom. The table
seems barely able to hold up this final freight.

Now I am back in school, every country in crayon color,
clear to the lowliest amateur. I am located, placed,
teacher's pet in the geography room (in any classroom)
where the steam radiators hiss their tropics
of naked freedom and lush nature, dissolving
common armor of long underwear for the wastes
of uncharted arctic elsewhere, where I have to go.
Here with what ease, what completeness, stretches every journey.
On such a globe any wandering brings you home.
In any nation each kindly native comes to meet you
with the same comprehensible greeting: "Take what I have to give you
with mind, feeling, imagination and my land is yours."
How full, how solid this most useful of human illusions!
Future highway maps lie in their flatness,
all four sides falling off into nothing,
and speak only in black lines of a foreign longhand,
but here one learns on faith, standing on tiptoe
to peep over cornfields, all the Principal Products,
and here the pastel paving of the seas can always be walked on
as if in those true blue fathoms there were nothing unfathomable after
    all,
as if there need be no capricious floes for Elizas to flee on,
as if there were no blinding salt, no hurricanes, no sinking.
This is a world the heart invented.

The Balloon Globe

The merest breath of a cooling fan
could displace this educational toy.
But the merest touch will roll it back.
Only my breath maintains its form.
But if it subsides I need only re-blow,
and as long as I breathe, I will—and so
when we go afar
no need to write, "Dear———————
wish you were here."
Here we always are.

THE FERRIS WHEEL

". . . that revolution that changed everything
and accomplished nothing." BRODKEY *on* BARTHES

It revolves, the great segmented seedpod,
slowly in the wind and dusk of the fairground
upon its unrelenting stem.
In each transparent cell an urgent pair
waits for the sense of a sprout, a tingle,
however tiny, of some transformation.

Pressed warmly close to him in foreknown enclosure,
she holds a grocery bag like a child on her lap,
cradling the only supper she was born to cook:
root vegetables that soften together into
a filling, bland companionship; gristly chunks
of that cheap flavor, essence of self
that any aging animal embodies;
a can of cayenne for the pinch that less and less often
startles to work the worn and dozing senses;
a bottle of babyfood purée for thickening—
the age-old stew that he may be by now,
for all she knows, heartily sick of.

As they are lifted she wonders at the unflagging
wish that brought them here again,
knowing what will be shown, wanting to see it.
Looking down, not upward, for the lights,
she sees the little constellation of a carnival
join, starspace by starspace, the whole community
of brightness until, for a timeless fraction of time,
her eyes flow over with a lighted heaven
on earth. Inexorably, she falls away
from such a sight and dwindles down
to strings of painted bulbs in a silly tangle . . .
and yet . . . before she can close her eyes
in loss the vision is already beginning to return.
And will withdraw. It is not to be teased

that the two of them have come, surely.
This is one of the world's most artful entertainments.

They rise. If it would stop at the top,
she thinks, words might replace our weight.
I am a woman, don't trust me, *tell* me,
she thinks. Does it remind you too
of the passionate climax, then the slow drift downward
into slums of sleep? If I were to speak
I might say (what would you say?) that, young, the heart
was humble camp-follower of the body's forays.
But fortunes change, and the prosperous and settled
give gracious hospitality to the poor.
Those briefest of all transcendences seem at last
the body's small, sweet hostess presents to the heart.

They rise again, but their playful teacher
stops and sways them gently near the peak.
She takes his hand. Recite with me, she presses
what so far we are jointly taking in.
Here, out of touch with everything but each other,
reality can indeed become romance.
The "land of dreams" can be as truthful a metaphor
as any "darkling plain"—the Wheel of our lives
has said so over and over,
(Do you believe that too?) and somehow in memory
might one bring down from the secret, sacred book
some fragments of clear translation, down
where the child pukes from its overdose of cotton candy
while the parents screech at each other, down
where even the starriest eye sees a fistfight raging
over some hennaed lady of the night,
where the unyielding longings clash
always with a world that will never yield?
Tell me how we can marry enthroned, imperious love
to common human kindness, in order to live
the only life worth living, the empathic life. . . .

They rise once more. Stop at the top, she thinks. They stop.
Within its frame of darkness in the infinite gallery
"earth hath not anything to show more fair."
She draws away from him, from his competent fists,
his fingers firmed by placards, voting levers,
hammer and tongs, steeringwheels, gavels,
avoids the eyes still fit for bombsights.
In this austere, private illumination
her own hands are being bound by soft cloths
(Beaute is Merciles) and she feels them cramp and wither.
She is held by a lover perfect in form and fire
before a symphony of signs, abstractions from rainbow,
lit rhyming in spaciousness of all things visible.
She can barely imagine now under the high finish
those specks that swarm and separate in confusion
the threat of their microscopic jaws
and of their heedless, cumulating excrements.
Don't sweep them away, she thinks in coldest charity
for that may leave a lasting stain
of formic acid on the masterpiece.
No, I have gone too far! Take me down!
Yet still, before she can return to everywhere,
heart in her mouth, she is force-fed the view.
"The heart's grown brutal from the fare."

(A last trip upward would be an anticlimax,
the Wheel being too worldly to speak to everything.
But if the stem should snap from a clumsy touch
of Nature's overpowering tropes, let it be said
that she counts on gravity to bring her back
finally, and for good, to the fairground.
Let my body land invisibly, she would think,
on top of the striking mallet that a boy
has swung to show his strength to his first scared girl
and help him ring for her that tinny bell.)

The Ferris Wheel

In the darker descent the highstrung bulbs
become more and more blinding. She thinks . . . still
. . . I still believe. . . . "Only connect!" she thinks . . .
"But what have I come to?" The exit platform.
She lifts her sack to leave and in the doorglass
by some great mirroring gift of the lights,
stronger than love, stranger than love,
she sees for life upon her own shoulders and neckstem
an image which replaces her own wherever she seeks it:
another's "tired, pleasure-hoping" face.

ON RECEIVING A POSTCARD FROM JAPAN

"If you can breakfast together," the gods said,
"(we've made up a little game) it will always be morning.
We've dammed back the tides of time and set a table
where the balked sea would whelm over with no warning."

Our beds were so far from each other that when I woke,
growing more ravenous with every scream,
I could not tear you with just an untouching voice
away from the lavish banquet of your dream.

Wanting the prize, fearing the dark water,
fighting the greedy senses, I tried to wait.
But as I sat starving the gods piled higher and higher
platters of fragrant temptations, and I ate.

Swimming and diving through the deep salt years,
wondering what you might be going to receive,
holding your breath, eyes stinging, feeling your way,
you came to the table I could not bear to leave.

But you'd grown gills from the long, passionate journey.
Smiling, you sit at ease on the gods' game-ground,
and in tender aqueous light of early morning
eat a late breakfast of sea-weed where I drowned.

THE BURNING OF YELLOWSTONE

Squaring their papers—tap, tap—the news team finds
one last feature to catch St. Louis ears
following days of rage and roar on the screen
as feather, fur, nest, cave, hide disappears.
"Don't miss the sunset tonight or tomorrow night!"
For two thousand miles, it appears, wind bore to the eye
smoke from unseen deaths and wounds to remind us
how beautiful, at the end, is the earth, the sky.
Driving west from the towers that block our view
we find a hillside pull-off. Every sense
confounded by the vision that wraps us round,
we feel to the bone its burning radiance.
Orange daylily uncurls its lips and presses
them urgently on the blue-veined brow of space.
Rose at its ripest spreads wide its fervent petals
to welcome the other hues. An intense trace
of crushed violet scent lies on the air.
Petunia tongues a pink both sweet and clear.
Fallout of deep red peony litters the treeline.
We take each other's hand, eyes wet, and hear
how gently the world informs its witnesses,
as jonquil yellow trumpets a floral boom,
of its debt to the artistry of their beholding,
of their culpability for its final bloom.

III

LINES WRITTEN IN A GUEST BOOK

For Tony and Helen, Masters of Many Arts

Both God and the gods in righteous anger hurled
calamitous bolts when hospitality
was bungled. All of us here now gratefully
count on the Hechts to save our clumsy world.

ADDENDUM FOR A FUTURE VISIT TO THE HECHT KITCHEN

"It's burnt!" cries the bride at a virgin feast
as she serves in tears the beloved guest,

and fears the fire whose glorious flare
can spoil what they both define as rare.

Amateur too, he shares her fear
that tenderness char, the sensitive sear

as leaping flames of passion and dread
whisk together their yellow and red.

Later, love goes to Gourmet School
and attempts a sophisticated drool

at the bite of a blackened fish filet—
a phase that quickly becomes passé

since out of depths comes a delicacy
too vital to lose to a pyre's decree.

Still later, more lasting, stronger, slimmer,
kept in stock at a constant simmer,

the past, the familiar bones and flesh
will make love's soup each day afresh—

though sometimes over banana or pear
romance like brandy will briefly re-flare.

But there's one more sweet we can serve each other
where wild warmth and calm are fused together.

Rich, dependable, pure, this food,
soft as custard from gratitude.

On the chill of knowing what is and is not,
friendship's broiler can't be too hot.

It's a classic dish that has come to stay,
so for life's pot-luck, here's a Heart Brulée.

ADDENDUM FOR A FUTURE VISIT TO THE HECHT STUDY

I
Someone once described the Japanese garden
as "trivialities arranged to look
significant." So might we label one kind
of poem, whose dry hint of a river or brook,
raked free of detritus, briefly flows, turns
into terraces (abstraction of waterfall)
and comes to its end in a large, strict rectangle
of the same white sand (the sea, the All
or Nothingness), whose stone showing its white
above the moss that wraps its lower part
can be read as a high mountain, forested
and snowcapped, in this metaphoric art.
Guided by its setting in white space
proportionally vast, the making mind

of the beholder, which walks hand in hand
with the austere creator, fast will find
one dwarf pine's looming. Shading, importance, meaning
tower from the green suggestion. Delicacy
molds throughout a narrow path between Nature's
carelessness and the lifeless rigidity
of perfect order. A world is here that returns
to pure idea when we look away,
its grasp on our hearts being as miniature
as the memory of one faultless, serene day.

II

But there is another kind of garden, another
poetry (might we say?) whose "mimicry
of endlessness" calls upon every muscle
of self, while the senses are whelmed toward idolatry.
To enter its rich acreage is to know
that much must be left for another day, or year
or season. Though Flora stands in stone, her kingdoms
of brilliant imagery cloud over or clear—
rosebeds, meadows of daffodil, rainbow
borders, wild blooms under treeshade—as time, as the sun,
changes their tourist. Next, breath-taking steeps and valleys;
then a Grotto for those the passage has undone,
attended by a kind-faced river-god.
Then, for sheer swagger, creation clipped to dream,
the topiary-work, the artist's little
joke on Nature, horse-play with be and seem.
Courage challenged, trusting the maker, one
may enter a Maze and step by step, deeper
into bewilderment, find in the yews
the cool and colder rehearsal of the sleeper
who loses in darkness time, place, others,
sense of self. But no, this is not that last
labyrinth of Minotaur or tomb,
and a string one hadn't noticed leads back fast,
the strong string that ties art to serious play.

And now the woods, where "art is used but to
conceal art." Light and dark and the dapple
of both are inside. Here and there a few
bright lines of birches sketch the merest hint
of happiness for all lost children, old
and young, scattering breadcrumbs in hope of home,
for lovers meeting in secret, Tristan, Isolde.
Strange, rare trees have been planted to look
at home with the colloquial. Deep
but penetrable, the woods release their guest,
having shown him beds of fern and heart's-ease they keep.
What loving lavishness creates such gardens—
worlds of thought and feeling as real as the world?
It is late. One stops and rests near a flowery fountain,
thinking with joy of what the tour unfurled,
thoughts that turn one's head toward a last far view,
the eye being led uphill by an aisle of green
between marbles of calm Athena and hurrying Eros
where the beautiful Folly of having lived can be seen.

THE INSIGHT LADY OF ST. LOUIS ON ZOOS

(a found oral poem)

The other day I had an insight.
I suddenly realized why I hate zoos.
You know how they build those enclosures
for an animal or two, and if the animal
is the kind that lives in a rocky country
they put one rock with it and then they say,
see, there it is in its natural habitat?
And if the animal is a forest animal
they plant one tree with it and then they say,
see, there it is in its natural habitat?
Well, the handyman had put up the new bookshelf
on the only wall in the house
that isn't already covered with bookshelves,
and I organized all the books I had used
to write my book on Svevo, and then
all the books I had used for my book on Kierkegaard,
and then I saw myself as a zoo animal.
They would build a bare room with three bare walls
and put me and one book in it and then they would say,
see, there she is in her natural habitat!

And that evening I went to a party
and when we left I went upstairs to get my own coat,
and you should have seen that upstairs—
how can people live in a mess like that?—
it looked as if the drugbusters had made a raid
and left every drawer half open
with the clothes and stuff dumped out on the floor,
and there was one book lying on the floor
and I picked it up to see what it was,
and then I had another terrible insight.
I knew what book they would put in my zoo pen.
It would be that book, *Building Bicycles*.

FOR DAVID KALSTONE

d. 1986

Chronos gathered the gods one day on their mountain.
"There is a man," he told them, "who pleases me
beyond most men. Look down at him and claim
your gifts to him as I name them, that I may see

how each of you shares his power with my precious mortals.
First, *Sweetness of nature*." A god began to beam.
"That was from me, I recognize my choice
of a vessel to fill from my coveted golden stream."

"*A manly gentleness*." A god looked down.
"Mine. I gave him the gift that would increase,
from my own nature, the chance for gods and men
to live in the dear community of peace."

"*Fealty to friends*." A war-like god
looked and spoke up. "Though battle needs my powers,
I know, and so gave him my gift for the linking of hands,
that fellowship offers the most immortal hours."

"*Brilliance of mind*." A god looked and with pride
cried out, "I found him worthy of *my* gold.
New-minted intelligence from my hoard I gave him,
subtle and sensitive and clear and bold."

"*Modesty*." A goddess claimed to have given
the most becoming raiment for all the years.
"*And a loving heart*." But that god could not look.
The eyes of Eros were blind with his own tears.

MISERS

for James Merrill

On the streets of New York I've seen them rummaging, the grizzled,
the torn, grimed and scabbed by the world, their mouths muzzled,

misers of crust and Coke bottle, whatever is valued or needed.
My unhelpful heart glints out at them, but is unheeded.

One man we free ones cherish is freer to reassess worth.
Miser of love and language, walking the streets of the earth,

he ransacks, ransoms what we all hold dear, then some days,
like someone who, out for a stroll, all Blackglama and Cartier,

with a collector's vision spots, in a streak of debris
on the sidewalk, a little length the poor can't use, dusty,

stranger still something unbarterable, absurd,
unneeded, unsought—like my heart or an archaic word—

he bends down and takes it, thinking, "I saw it, it is mine."
Only the rich—the gifted—know how to treasure Twine.

JOURNAL JOTTINGS

I

Along each one-hour segment of the unimaginable
length of a sand and briar trail of love,
one doctor, like the dusky Bushman tracker,
sights a new footprint
Wind will soon shift the sand to cover it,
but not before vision photographs
inklings of form and pressure invisible
to all but that aboriginal eye,
saving and using the nearly forgotten secret:
"No two human beings step the same."

II

Meanwhile from snarl and smogsweat of emotional cities,
doctors dressed in billboard and streetsign direct the crowds
first to auto dispensaries for more speed and ease,
then onto the track-free highway of the Viennese.

III

As a poet (Howard Moss
in *Whatever Is Moving*) wrote:
"People who are summed up in a word
are people we are lying about."

IV

But how, in the dark muddle of the Marabars,
can we bear what happens, what we feel and hear?
How can we make our mindful entrance merely
an excursion without dreadful consequences?
Fiction holds up a torch of motivation.
Cause can be comprehended; in that light
no one but the aroused imagination
is with Adela, and in the sociable mob
what smothers Mrs. Moore is sweet new life,

the bare foot of a baby's innocence.
Mystery stories muffle the *ou-boum*
with tiny ear-plug answers to every why.

Yet, using fiction, Forster destroys these fictions.
Over and over we must burn his book
to go on thinking in a comfortable West,
to forget the India of the chaotic heart.

v

Another novelist (Stanley Elkin), remembering,
says to a friend: "There are moments
when the sheer wonder of man's
ability to join with man in one endeavor
transcends belief.
In a concert hall I never hear
the first note of a symphony
without tears coming to my eyes."

COTTON WAGONS

Down highways walled with green, both leafed and pine,
we drove south in late October to Oxford.
From Rowan Oak, where the small man Faulkner
slept in his small bed (but later Miss Welty's friend
told us Jill took the furniture, what's there now
is "of the period"), we took a county road,
the radiant fields of cotton blooms in their purply leaf-bed
running unfenced right to the side of the car.
Acres of bright white flowers on either side of the road,
with here and there a picking machine and a wagon
in the field, the wagons wire-netted between their spaced
thin boards. Down the road in the hot fall sun
we drove behind a filled wagon throwing
its puffs of white all over the road like popcorn.
The road and its rims were covered with white
from the passage of wagons as if it had heavily hailed.

Then heydays of hot spiced crabs and raw oysters,
carpenter's lace and wrought-iron lace,
Hallowe'en masqueraders and jazz,
a bayou cruise and dark roast coffee in New Orleans.

Driving north to home the highway walls are mottled
with red, orange and yellow in the evergreen.
An icy wind thumps away at the little car.
We catch up with and follow a white-filled cotton wagon
popping its white on either side to the wind.
"What are those spots of red in the cotton?" We pass.
"Oh God, not cotton!" Feathers snow on our windows.
White chickens are mashed together in layered pens,
the sides wire-netted between the spaced thin boards,
the freezing wind ripping away their feathers
and plastering big red combs flat on their heads
like bloody wigs. A wagonload of suffering,
silent as cotton. "Drive faster, get away!"
The wagon passes us. Again a snow

of ripped-off feathers. "Pass it, I can't stand it!"
We crash the speed limit and leave it behind,
but can't leave behind the rocketing hearts,
the pain of the wind, the red-flecked white silence.
I think of the fryer in my freezer, my recipe
for mixing five-spice powder and soya in a paste.
I rub the paste on the cold skin with my fingers.

THE BLOCK

Childless, we bought the big brick house on the block,
just in case. We walked the dog. Mornings the women
looked up from their clipping and pruning and weeding
to greet us, at dusk the men stopped their mowing to chat.
The children were newly married or off to college,
and dogs they had left behind them barked from backyards
at our dog, first in warning, later in greeting.
On other blocks we walked in the zany blare
of adolescent records and stepped around skates
and tricycles left on the sidewalk, but our middle-aged block,
busy and quiet, settled us into its solace.

The years bloomed by. The old dogs were put to sleep.
We bought a scoop to walk our new pup on his leash
as the block turned newly cranky about its curbs.
A lucky few dragged a staggering grandchild on visit
up and down, shyly accepting praise.
The wife on the corner shovelled their snow. "They say
it's what kills the men. I won't take a chance with my husband."
Then bad news began to come, hushed voices passed it
across back fences, the job of collecting for plants
found its permanent volunteer on the block. Later
more flowers, and one left alone in some of the houses.
Salads and cakes and roasts criss-crossed the street.

Then the long, warm, secret descent began
and we slid along with it. "We need a last dog," I said,
"but I can't face it." My husband became the husband
of the widows on either side in his husbandly tasks
of lifting and drilling for pictures and fixing faucets,
and a kindly old handyman took over, house by house,
the outdoor chores of mowing and small repairs.
"What would we do without Andrew?" everyone said.
The graying children came oftener, checking on things.
One widower wanted to marry the widow next door,
but "I'm through with *that* business!" she told him. The lone lesbian

kept up her house, but nearly wrinkled away.
I turned my flower borders to beds of groundcover.

The end came before we knew it. All in one year
my husband retired and half of the houses emptied.
Cancer ate four, heart attacks toppled some others,
a nursinghome closed over one, the rest caned off
to apartments with elevators. For Sale signs loomed
like paper tombstones on the weedy lawns.
The gentle years turned vicious all of a sudden.
"I can't believe it," we said. "The block's gone.
No one buys houses now." Those of us left
drew close, exchanged keys "in case something happens."
The wealthy patriarch sat all day on his porch
across the street and watched the distant disaster.
"He's way in his nineties," our busybody reported.
"His day and night nurses keep leaving, he's so awful.
And he won't take his pills. He just says, 'What does it matter?' "

We left on a long vacation. Home to the block,
we saw For Sale signs gone, heard new dog voices.
Bedding plants sucked up color from the old soil.
"The block is filled with young families. Everything's changed,"
we heard right away. A flyer stuck in the door:
"Block Party Sunday. Street Blocked Off All Day.
Bring Something To Share. All Bikes and Trikes Are Welcome."
"Oh Lord, do we have to go to all that bedlam?"
my husband said. "Oh God, I think they eat
hot dogs or something like that," I said. Too late,
Time, in its merciless blindness, gave us children.

THE ACCUSATION

I accuse the earth of uncaring.
It has learned a lie from its grass,
which repeats itself when it's slain,
saying uncountedly in its thin,
dainty, implacable voice,
"I am green, I am here, here is green,"
from its forests, which are cut down
and wait through the briery claim
of wild raspberry bush to the sun
for the alder thicket's protection
and then make their towering return.
It has learned to think only en masse.
It is sloven, without sift or choice,
and puts on what time tosses in bolts
of genus and species, and belts
of groundcover in clashes with beads
and bows of bugs and bacilli
capped off with drouths and floods
that kill the effect of the whole,
and with self-satisfaction parades
in whatever life it is wearing.

I charge us all with uncaring.
We have learned a lie from the earth,
the sweetened statistical lie
which allows newscasters to read
in their cheery, businesslike way,
"In a fire ten children are dead
and that story is certainly sad,"
and "THIRTY-FIVE MILLION TO END"
because there is not enough food
ninety universes away
from the paper we hold in our hand
as if they were fields of hay.
The more lost, the less each is worth.
With the gravest misunderstanding,

since they've taken earth's story to tell,
fictionists multiply endings,
steering clear of the "Little Nell"
that accedes to our curious hurt,
while the cannons of number drown out
each heart in its hutch of bone
which whispers when somebody's gone
he is one, irreplaceably one,
and that this is pain beyond bearing.

How can human love be unfearing?
The triumphant spawn of the earth
that transcends its own feckless dam
can be blistered to death by the same
giant magnifying glass
of empathy over the brain
and the heart in its hutch of bone
that keeps it from seeding like grass
and tells it instead to aim
its one billion sperm at one chosen
ovum and one alone
and to seed the concept of worth.
But how beautiful is the outfit
of life that the earth is wearing
when seen in such touching detail
of herb-tassel, bird-feather and paw-print,
head-horn, hide-mottle—one handful
of the sentient threads of the whole!
One bud can be apprehended.
One broken wing can be mended,
for no lie can conceal the truth
that our kind was built to be caring.

MOCKINGBIRD MONTH

A pupa of pain, I sat and lay one July,
companioned by the bird the Indians called "four hundred
tongues." Through the dark in the back yard by my bed,
through the long day near my front couch, the bird
sang without pause an amplified song "two-thirds
his own," books told me, "and one-third mimicry."

Gray charmer, "the lark and nightingale in one,"
unremitting maker of music so full of wit
and improvisation, I strained by night and light
to hear the scientists' record: "In ten minutes
he mimicked thirty-two species." I counted eight
(even I) variations on cardinal's song alone.

Cock of the neighborhood, his white flashes of wing
and long distinguished tail ruled the bushes and boughs,
and once, enchanted, I saw him walk past my house,
herding, from three feet behind, the neighbor's nice,
cowardly cat. He controlled without any fuss
but took little time off. Most of our month he sang.

The sticky wings of my mind began to open.
No mere plagiarist, a Harold Bloom singer,
he leaned on, but played with, robin or jay or
starling or whippoorwill. I began to prefer
him and house and hurting to the world outdoors.
Both art and art-lover attend to what may happen.

The weeks went by. At two A.M. he'd begin
my steadier, stronger, surer flight through his airs,
and the sun sent us into heights of his lyric together.
Virtuoso though he was, I was learning his repertoire.
Who would have thought the moth of me would tire?
Toward the end of a month in concert I began to complain.

Constant cadence, I told him, gives one no rest.
Is it my fault you must be lonesome for a mate?
There must be no nestlings to feed (when do *you* eat?).
What master of complexity won't duplicate
with incessant singing? Delete, delete, delete,
shut up for a while my bird-brained, brilliant stylist!

I left him for the North and less prolific birds
(but not before reading a chatty chapter on him
by a man who threw a shoe treeward at four A.M.
to stop "that endless torrent"), my movement a handsome
tribute to his voice. Leaving my pencils at home,
I resolved to husband my own apprentice words.

TEARS

All spring the grim machines ground out the verdict:
Cause Unknown For These Eyes' Misbehaving,
and the sprightly doctor leaped from guess to guess,
from pill to potion said to be sight-saving.
Through the latest lens, crying (and laughing too),
I read and re-read the book of a friend, then went
to the next appointment. "Another test." He pasted
tabs of paper on the eyeballs, bent
the lids to cover them, and left, later
peeled them from the red rage of each eye.
"Negative," he mourned. "You have plenty of tears!"
Positively, I'd not used up my supply.

Preferring mystery to science, eyes
returned to normal without explanation.
Words brought their message to me from the others,
light or dark, open or shy. No need to ration
sweet salve of empathy that from the corners
of vision on hurt hearts comes soothing and seeping.
Its having been threatened by sudden paper clues,
I held more dear the privilege of weeping
than ever in cloudburst youth. That gentle rain
is more than mercy, though twice-blessed indeed,
being the very signal of human love,
or so I told myself. With brutal speed
this wisdom of song and story met its match,
and science, once balked, more than made up arrears.
"DON'T CRY IN AN OPEN WOUND," news headlines blazoned.
"AIDS-RELATED VIRUS FOUND IN TEARS!"

A BOUQUET OF ZINNIAS

One could not live without delicacy, but when
I think of love I think of the big, clumsy-looking
hands of my grandmother, each knuckle a knob,
stiff from the time it took for hard grasping
with only my childhood's last moment for the soft touch.
And I think of love this August when I look
at the zinnias on my coffee table. Housebound
by a month-long heat wave, sick simply of summer,
nursed by the cooler's monotone of comfort,
I brought myself flowers. a sequence of multicolors.
How tough they are, how bent on holding their flagrant
freshness, how stubbornly in their last days instead
of fading they summon an even deeper hue
as if they intended to dry to everlasting,
and how suddenly, heavily, they hang their heads at the end.
A "high prole" flower, says Fussell's book on American
class, the aristocrat wouldn't touch them, says Cooper
on class in England. So unguardedly, unthriftily
do they open up and show themselves that subtlety,
rarity, nuance are almost put to shame.
Utter clarity of color, as if amidst all that
mystery inside and outside one's own skin
this at least were something unmistakeable,
multiplicity of both color and form, as if
in certain parts of our personal economy
abundance were precious—these are their two main virtues.

In any careless combination they delight.
Pure peach-cheek beside the red of a boiled beet
by the perky scarlet of a cardinal by flamingo pink
by sunsink orange by yellow from a hundred buttercups
by bleached linen white. Any random armful
of the world, one comes to feel, would fit together.
They try on petal shapes in public, from prim scallops
to coleslaw shreds of a peony heart, to the tousle
of a football chrysanthemum, to the guilelessness

of a gap-toothed daisy, and back to a welter
of stiff, curved dahlia-like quills. They all reach out.

It has been a strange month, a month of zinnias.
As any new focus of feeling makes for the mind's
refreshment (one of love's multitudinous uses),
so does a rested mind manage to modify
the innate blatancy of the heart. I have studied these blooms
who publish the fact that nothing is tentative
about love, have applauded their willingness to take
love's ultimate risk of being misapprehended.
But there are other months in the year, other levels
of inwardness, other ways of loving. In the shade
in my garden, leaf-sheltering lilies of the valley,
for instance, will keep in tiny, exquisite bells
their secret clapper. And up from my bulbs will come
welcome Dutch irises whose transcendent blue,
bruisable petals curve sweetly over their center.

I V

GLAD HEART AT THE SUPERMARKET

Still more regimented than the daily runs
are your trips to the supermarket. The tense hunts
on cans and cartons for additives, dyes, animal
fats and coconut oils, all the grabbing at once
for oat bran waffles and oat bran English muffins,
the orchestrated turning of backs on caffeine,
red meat, salt, sugar, butter, eggs,
finding the fish oil capsules, the Lean Cuisine,
the complex carbohydrates—pasta in salad or box.
As yet only two of you collapsed, I've heard,
into supermarket neurosis, one mate has rebelled
at the low cholesterol of too much bean curd.
Dear friends, dear aging hearts that are stressed by young
surges and shocks of feeling, dear minds aquiver,
their stiffening vessels bulged with the rush of fresh
insights, jokes, dreams, may you live forever!
But let me taste, while I'm here, the new flavors
of otherness in your changing cases and shelves,
plucking with free, unguarded gluttony
that keeps my tongue in spiced surprise at your selves.
For we die of sameness too, or die to each other.
Familiarity, like a child, may fold
a monstrous lettuce leaf and cut away
till flat, green folk, unfolded, are holding hands,
then serve that undressed salad of friends each day.

Abundance! Incalculable abundance in each
of you may I shop among. Once I found
your image in a dream-like, time-pressed tour
of foreign Food Halls—cathedral-high, profound
in the mystery of the not-yet-served-or-tasted.
I glimpsed warm pigeon salad with walnuts, wild
boar, roe deer and hare patés, quail mousse,
rosepetal vinegar. Wealth-dazed, beguiled
by one glance at a take-out dish called "Love in Disguise"—
a calf's heart coated with vermicelli and breadcrumb,

Glad Heart at the Supermarket

I saw ahead a darkened aisle, roped off:
the sacred privacy where no one should come.
(Store-room of the I, where secret recipes
and orders go forth to the world outside the skin,
is as dark, perhaps, to the I as to anybody,
and love is least likely to lighten the deepest bin.)
For the sweet quotidian your supermarkets
more than suffice. They're dependable—I know
what each one stocks—yet at unexpected times
new ices, canned goods or sea-foods are put on show.
I know where to reach for what, but a joy of friendship
is the strange savor that answers to no felt lack.
Even the steadfast store that I know best,
the closest to me, brought forth a few years back
the kiwi I'd never tasted; one day the first
tang of arugula appeared. No treat
in mind today, I picked out produce I needed.
Something called jicama rolled and fell at my feet.

CONDEMNED SITE

Peter, Tom, David, Jim and Howard are gone.
Down hallways, in long-kept rooms, four others are in danger.
In Love's old boardinghouse the shades of five rooms are drawn.

At table their places are set, their tea-time kettle is on,
no space has been aired and emptied for the needy stranger,
though Peter, Tom, David, Jim and Howard are gone.

No one answers the ring of phone, the knocks from dusk to dawn
of Sorrow's cost-accountant, the would-be rearranger
of Love's old boardinghouse. The shades of five rooms are drawn

on the Heart's unlicensed embalming. Soon, fenced from the lawn,
only the watching world, privacy's dog-in-the-manger,
can say Peter, Tom, David, Jim and Howard are gone,

and even the world, turning, will glimpse them alive in a spawn
of unchanging images they tore from Time, the changer.
In Love's old boardinghouse the shades of five rooms are drawn,

but those rooms are bright and warm. Four other guests are in danger
in Love's old boardinghouse. The shades of five rooms are drawn
as if Peter, Tom, David, Jim and Howard were gone.
A house of shades is crumpled by Life, the great Stock Exchanger.

MEMOIR

for Harry Ford

As the conch tells the human ear,
silence wants to be sound,
so the earshell beseeches the eye
to find the sounds it would lose,
and the eye prays that flying words
will be trapped in the amber of print.

Like a pine the man who will print
what plays through his needle-branched ear
towers, his resin wraps words
and the resonant shape of their sound
that a dry heart has to let loose.
He will pass through art's strict needle's eye.

When the poem arrives at the eye
of the hurricane, hush of print
retrieves what the blind wind would lose.
Then the heart becomes all ear
and the deaf-mute world hears the sound
of its own green, resplendent words.

Who gives up the world for words
gives creation a bad black eye
in uncoupling sense and sound.
Detective Time takes his voiceprint,
which ends behind bars. Nature's ear
knows it was little to lose.

The heart must be mud-mum or lose
face when the god without words,
with child-cheeks, with Orphic ear,
lies down there, shuttered of eye,
and leaves his indelible imprint.
Love's incoherence is sound.

In a deathly silence, what sound
amends Time's law that we lose?
That memoir read from fine print,
love's beautiful babble its Foreword,
while art fixes the world I-to-eye.
Then breath beats the drum of our ear.

Sound ear and sound eye keep in print
any rhyme the world makes with its words
that the heart cannot bear to lose.

LAST WORDS OF PIG NO. 6707

> *"The pig with human genes seldom gets up. The boar,*
> *bigger-snouted and hairier than usual, lies in his pen*
> *despite the nudgings of a normal pig put in for com-*
> *pany. Pig No. 6707 is unlike any other. He is a prom-*
> *ising subject from the U.S. Department of Agricul-*
> *ture's experiments transplanting human genes into farm*
> *animals. . . . The main goal of these experiments has yet*
> *to be achieved. The scientists are trying to . . . create*
> *'super animals'. . . . Some side effects of the gene trans-*
> *fer trouble the scientists. Pig No. 6707 and some of the*
> *others in the experiments lie on their sides much of the*
> *time with their eyes closed. They are too lethargic to*
> *stand, let alone mate. . . ."*
>
> The St. Louis Post-Dispatch, Dec. 8, 1986

The width of one of my bristles lies between
desire and do for him who wallows in
his wishes, bumps me with a fellow flesh
he barely knows the limits of, while I
in the muddied have so muddling far to go.
At least someone is with me. He swills the world,
pigpen I came to life in, and in a gushy
answer it rushes into our trough. Soap
and soup, turd and tenderloin, bone and banana,
acorn and angelcake are ground to one gulp
his gut says Bravo to. His happiness hogs our ground
as I try merely to sift the sweet from the savorless.
Someone is with me who does not need me as I
need him, who never lies alone hide-to-hide.
My snout swells out with all that might be said.
Grief, praise: one grunt, even under the brilliant
pupil of this wide blue eye of sky?

That focus from above seems only careful
to my companion, pledge to his roly-poly
of comfort, corn, consciousness. Beam back,
he feels when warm it falls on his broad-beamed back.

But I, I, grounded, can't bear the blinding vision
of my days: out of the round red center
of all of overhead spread bright orange strings
like spokes, like tent-ribs tethered to earth's edges,
making a monstrous spiderweb, world-wide.
Black against the blue background, a being
tightropes his way along the lengths of glow,
feeling along the unseen strands that link them,
teeters, toeing lifelong, never knowing which
are the sticky rays, but knowing Soon? Later?

—it's *me*! Into his parlor, sooner or later
I'll come, cold parlor of the pest of the world.
I see it always, except when my eyelids close
and my pig-headed dream projects itself again.
In it I wait in the hot-seat, center, the great web
sways like a hammock, as if my weight were wind.
A tremble! I trot unmired on the radiant line
I know, bundle with artful filaments
the iridescent, dear, green- and gold-glittering
fly. Held live, he is essence, famine-food
I do not hog. I deck the web with him,
he and kindred dangle, glint like crystals
on that one-orbed chandelier. Lift lids?
Lose place-and face-saving limelight? Eye the sty?

I lie blinkered, bright-eyed inside. Why do they
fill me with their fierce, first-born claims,
the others? Pig, primrose, peanut—the packed world
wants more space, space in my very skin.
Jaws clenched against them, somehow I swallowed whole.
My heart rips where they root for their own rarity,
sumptuous truffle they turn up there. Friend,
frater who nudges me toward norm, how can I,
sick with others' senses, mate, create,
when what seems a ton of mere simple caritas
sandbags my streams? In my stuffed porkrind you too

Last Words of Pig No. 6707

    snooze, squeal, live, beautiful polished
    pigskin air-filled with the unequivocal.
    Kick you out? I hear the green globe grieve
    for any image lost in its purposeless play.
    You are lean, lardless compared to me, can lift
    the self up. I am fat with fellows, failings, figments . . .

    I give the glebe back this weight, this heaviness . . .
    O god of the ground, I am so *heavy* with what
    my tiny trotters were surely not built to bear!

HEADLINES

The great black bellow tells us together
to be moved, to move. Interlocked into
a mega-jigsaw puzzle, rigid
as tenet, we begin a glacial slide
that crushes contours, countries, carries us
to importance, from daily to the eternal.
The Big Picture, we model behind us
mountains of death, foothills of hunger,
meadows of merriment, chasms and cliffs
of power and helplessness, ice-lock
the free-running life of the mind. We move
in grandeur to the meltdown. There,
lines of a global banner hail us,
tell, in words we can no longer read,
the history of what we were.

In lowercase titter, agony columns
confide to the you, the me, that style
alone is serious. In darkness
we sneak to that Theater Schadenfreude
where, tied to the tracks, self-respect
in foolish ruffles and pantaloons
awaits the next episode. Romance,
whose feet in bed smell to high heaven,
is complained of by Constant Wife, while achill
in her trite Teddies, the Other Woman
poses outside to understand him.
Each morning ambition shaves off by finger
a lather of custard pie. Between
each feature the animated cartoon
of caritas as a permanent,
ridiculous adolescent plays.
When butterfingers drops the hot rock
of the heart from any ledge to the stream
of the life of the mind below, which goes up
in steam, then even Time's blind date

turns out to be a transsexual
and we all go home. There, on its forehead,
the artless mirror outlines our story:
There's no lifestyle for the feelings, yet
it's deathless, that trivial blazoning.

DOUBLE SONNET FOR MINIMALISTS

The spiral shell
apes creamhorns of smog,
Dalmation, quenelle
or frosted hedgehog,
yet is obsessed
by a single thought
that its inner guest
is strictly taught.

When the self that grew
to follow its rule
is gone, and it's through,
vacant, fanciful,

its thought will find
Fibonacci's mind.

That fragile slug,
bloodless, unborn,
till it knows the hug
of love's tutoring form,
whose life, upstart
in deep, is to learn
to follow the art
of turn and return,

when dead, for the dense
casts up no clue
to the infinite sequence
it submitted to.

May its bright ghost reach
the right heart's beach.

SONNET FOR MINIMALISTS

From a new peony,
my last anthem,
a squirrel in glee
broke the budded stem.
I thought, where is joy
without fresh bloom,
that old hearts' ploy
to mask the tomb?

Then a volunteer
stalk sprung from sour
bird-drop this year
burst in frantic flower.

The world's perverse,
but it could be worse.

NOTES

At the New Orleans Zoo: Facts and quotations in this poem are taken from Cynthia Moss, *Portraits in the Wild*, Houghton Mifflin, Boston, 1975.

Near Changes: Mario Vargas Llosa, "Is Fiction the Art of Lying?" The New York Times Book Review, October 7, 1984.

The Ferris Wheel: This poem was written, not out of, but along-side, so to speak, the scene in Graham Greene's *The Third Man* where Harry Lime talks to his friend Martins on the Wheel. When it stops at the highest point there is a passage from which I have borrowed, for a quite different purpose, several phrases: " 'Oh, I still *believe*, old man. In God and Mercy and all that. I'm not hurting anyone's soul by what I do. The dead are happier dead. They don't miss much, poor devils,' he added with that odd touch of genuine pity, as the car reached the platform and the faces of the doomed-to-be-victims, the tired, pleasure-hoping Sunday faces, peered in at them."

Double Sonnet For Minimalists: Fibonacci discovered that spirals in nature take a form that can be described by an infinite sequence of numbers, in which each one is the sum of the two preceding ones. Biologists tell us that in the spiral shell the slug within is spiral, whereas a slug without a shell is never spiral. The shell teaches the slug its form.

A NOTE ABOUT THE AUTHOR

Mona Van Duyn (Mrs. Jarvis Thurston) was born in Waterloo, Iowa in 1921 and since 1950 has lived in St. Louis. She has taught at the University of Iowa Writers' Workshop, the University of Louisville, Washington University, The Salzburg Seminar in American Studies and at Breadloaf and various other writers' workshops around the United States. With her husband she founded *Perspective, a Quarterly of Literature* in 1947 and co-edited it until 1970. She has received the Eunice Tietjens Award (1956) and the Harriet Monroe Award (1968) from *Poetry*, the Helen Bullis Prize (1964) from *Poetry Northwest*, the National Book Award (1971) and The Bollingen Prize (1970). In 1976 she received the Loines Prize from the National Institute of Arts and Letters and in 1983 was elected a member of that body. In 1980 she was voted the Fellowship of the Academy of American Poets and became a Chancellor of the Academy in 1985. She was one of the first five American poets to be given a grant from the National Foundation for the Arts, and held a Guggenheim Fellowship for 1972–1973. In 1987 she received the Shelley Memorial Prize from the Poetry Society of America and in 1989 the Ruth Lilly Prize from *Poetry* and the American Council on the Arts. Washington University and Cornell College awarded her the degree of Honorary Doctor of Letters.

A NOTE ON THE TYPE

This book was set on the Linotype in Janson, a recutting made direct from type cast from matrices long thought to have been made by the Dutchman Anton Janson, who was a practicing type founder in Leipzig during the years 1668–1687. However, it has been conclusively demonstrated that these types are actually the work of Nicholas Kis (1650–1702), a Hungarian, who most probably learned his trade from the master Dutch type founder Dirk Voskens. The type is an excellent example of the influential and sturdy Dutch types that prevailed in England up to the time William Caslon (1692–1766) developed his own incomparable designs from them.

Composition by Heritage Printers, Inc.
Charlotte, North Carolina
Printing and binding by Halliday Lithographers,
West Hanover, Massachusetts